# Once Upon a Rhythm

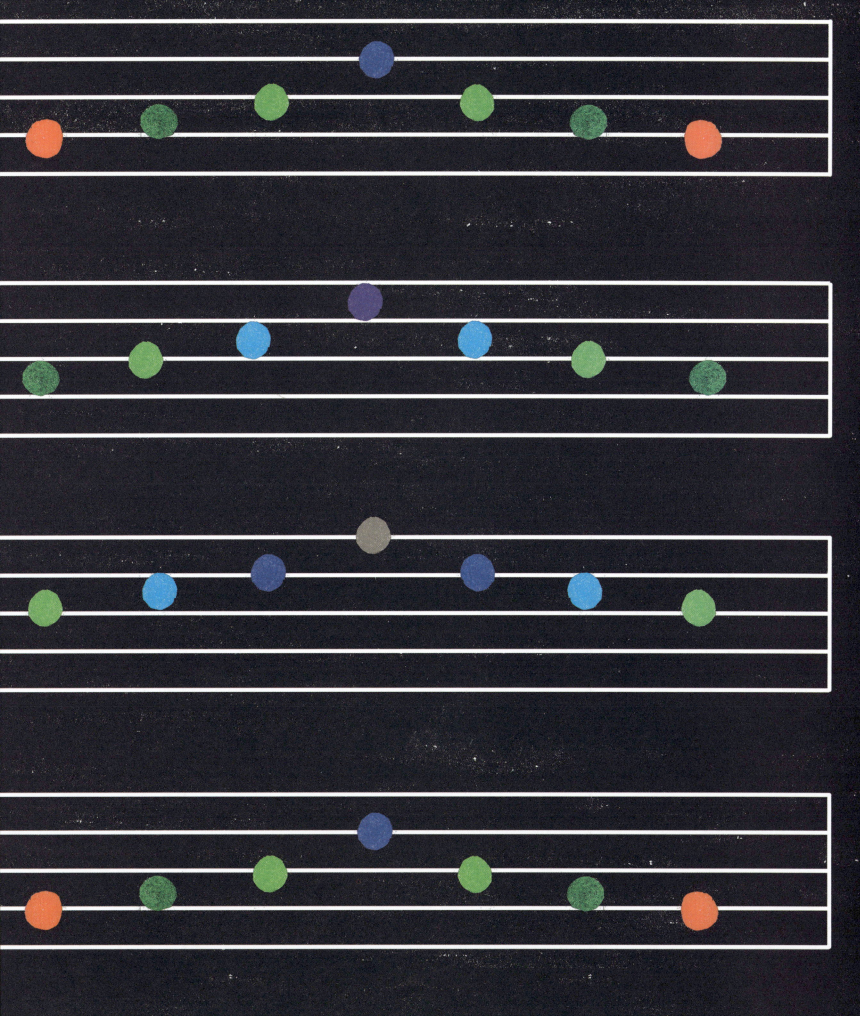

With all my love for Madeleine C,
one brimful with musicality
~ James Carter

To Gabriel, Jaqueline and Alexander

~ Valerio Vidali

**CATERPILLAR BOOKS**
An imprint of the LITTLE TIGER GROUP
1 Coda Studios, 189 Munster Road, London SW6 6AW
Imported into the EEA by Penguin Random House Ireland,
Morrison Chambers, 32 Nassau Street, Dublin,
D02 YH68 • www.littletiger.co.uk
First published in Great Britain 2019
This edition published in 2021
Text copyright © James Carter 2019
Illustrations copyright © Valerio Vidali 2019
A CIP catalogue record for this book
is available from the British Library
All rights reserved • ISBN: 978-1-83891-171-3
Printed in China • CPB/1400/1693/0121
2 4 6 8 10 9 7 5 3 1

# Once
# Upon
# a
# Rhythm

## The Story of Music

**James Carter**

Illustrated by **Valerio Vidali**

LITTLE TIGER

LONDON

# Boom!

## What's that?
## Boom! That thing?

It's there as you **walk**

as you **dance** as you **sing**.

# Boom! Your drum!
## Boom! Your beat!

It starts in your **heart**

then it spreads to your **feet.**

There's a **rhythm** out there
there's a **rhythm** within
as the **seasons** turn
as the **planets** spin.

It's the **call of the wild**
it's the **breath of the world**
and it's **life so alive**
that it has to **be heard**.

And it hums and it thrums
through day and night
it's the **magical**, **mystical**

# rhythm of life!

Let's follow our music – follow it back
but how did it start? With a stomp or a clap?
With songs we chanted? Songs we sang?
Somehow in Africa music began...

Things we **built and played by hand**
like **drums with skins** would cross the sands.

**Rhythms would strike** on tools of stone
and notes would trail from **flutes of bone.**

Communal songs
by old were sung
and so were heard
and learnt by young.

Wherever we settled
new instruments came
new melodies, harmonies
rhythms would play…

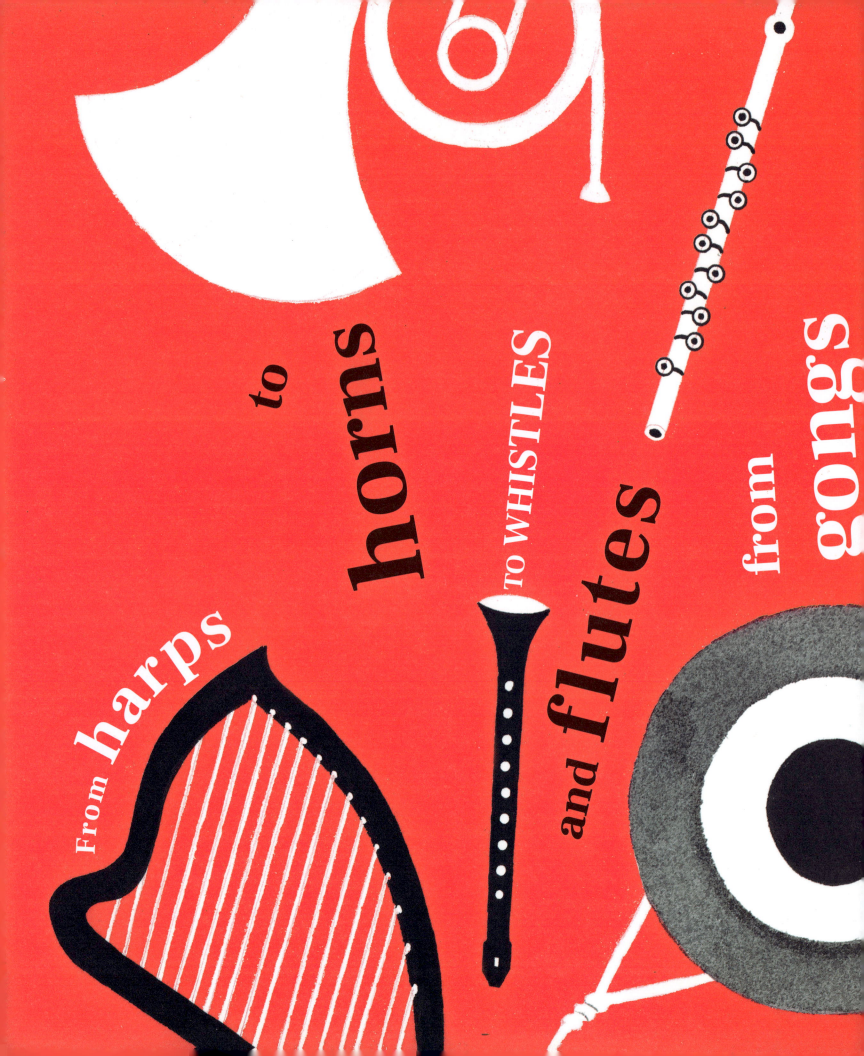

From **harps** to **horns** TO WHISTLES and **flutes** from **gongs**

And so, in time  we finally found

a way to **write**

our music down.

Squiggly **notes**

on five long lines

so we could play from

**musical signs.**

Now rivers of rhythms
across the globe

would colour the air
would pulse, would flow

Musical forms appeared anew
**classical, folk** and **choral** too.

Orchestras, choirs
all kinds of bands

journeyed around
**across the lands**.

# Jazz to country, samba to swing
### many new styles, new songs to sing.

Rap to pop to rock 'n' roll
Afrobeat to dub to soul.

Electric guitars went
**jangle 'n' twang**
The singers went YEAH!
**The drums went BANG!**

Gigs and festivals

needed more sound

we turned it up

to LOUDER than LOUD!

# Boom! That rhythm! Boom! It's you!

# Hey, **you** could be a **musician**, too!

# Listen to life's

**R**hythm has always been important to us. About 100,000 years ago, we began clapping, stamping and weaving songs into our everyday lives.

**H**istorians tell us that the first instruments were probably drums, some 40,000 years ago. They were used for rituals and celebrations and communicating between villages. Music is a great way of bringing people together.

**Y**ou would be amazed at the range of traditional instruments – from the harp-like African *kora* to the haunting Indian *sitar*, and from the mournful Irish *uilleann* pipes to the majestic Arabic *oud* from North Africa.

**T**oday, music can be recorded onto a CD, MP3, vinyl record or tape, and we can listen to it on radios, phones or computers. Not that long ago it had to be written down to be preserved – a system devised in Greece and Syria in around 6000BCE.

**H**undreds of years ago, there were only really two forms of music: classical and folk. Nowadays, there are many. Most musicians agree that whatever the genre, the best way to hear music is when it's played live.

**M**usic is now taught in schools, colleges and universities. You can study how to play almost any instrument, from the saxophone to the synthesiser, the banjo to the double bass. Which one would you like to learn...?

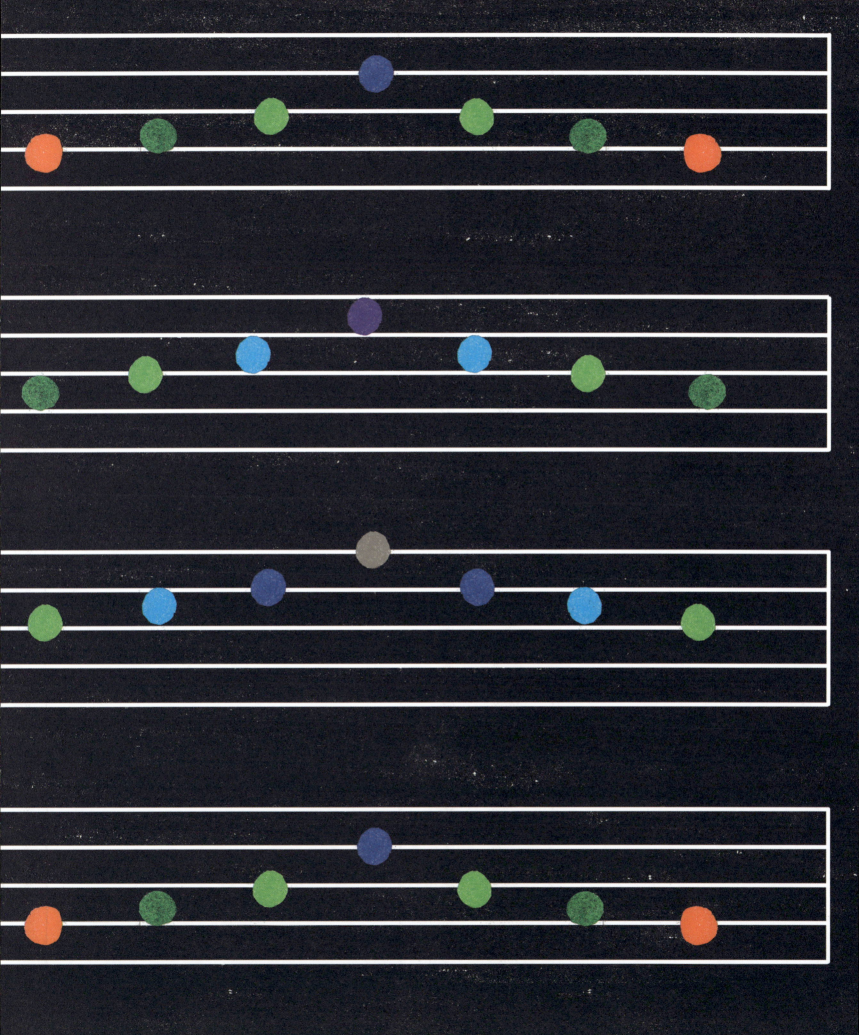